THE **CREATOR'S** JOURNAL

THE **CREATOR'S** JOURNAL

ERIC THAYNE

Niche Pressworks
Indianapolis

THE CREATOR'S JOURNAL

ISBN
Hardcover: 978-1-962956-23-9
Paperback: 978-1-962956-22-2

Published by Niche Pressworks, Indianapolis, IN
NichePressworks.com

Printed in the United States of America

THE CREATOR'S JOURNAL

CONTENT CREATION IS A PERSONAL DEVELOPMENT JOURNEY.

IN *CREATE DON'T CAPTURE,* I tell the story of how content creation saved not only my business, but in a way, also my life. It was this simple practice of creating content every day, building an audience of like-minded people, and creating products for them that multiplied my business and helped me achieve success and a lifestyle that few people experience.

I've often said that the most rewarding and beneficial result of creating content consistently is not the likes, the followers, or the money. Rather, it's that through this process you will truly figure out who you are. When you commit to adopting the identity of a creator, sharing yourself with the world, and creating value for your audience, it will send you on a journey of self discovery. You will gain clarity on your message and your calling. You'll gain a deeper understanding of yourself—your values, morals, beliefs, opinions, and ideals.

And the more you do that, the better your brand and content will become. Your content will feel more real and authentic. It will be more fun and fulfilling to create. Your audience will resonate on a deeper level with you and what you do. You will gain followers at an accelerated pace. And people will love buying from you.

Most importantly though, your life, business, content, and audience will all be in complete alignment with you, your strengths, and what makes you unique. And that combination will make you unstoppable. Instead of fighting against yourself, you'll be able to lean into your natural operating system and live in a constant state of creative flow. And you'll be able to grow (your business, your audience, and in your life) much faster because of it.

This journal is designed to help facilitate that process. As you use this journal, you will find that you gain greater clarity on who you are and what you're about, but you'll also find that it helps you create better content, spread more unique, interesting ideas, and grow your business as an entrepreneur.

This isn't simply a place to write down your thoughts every night, but rather it's an entire process that will benefit your life in many ways. When you commit to this process, it will help you:

- Sleep better
- Gain clarity on your goals and vision
- Understand yourself better
- Create better content
- Live in abundance
- Prioritize your workload
- Be more productive
- Find more fulfillment in your work

All of these results are necessary to truly live and operate in the mindset of a "creator". And when you do, you'll find that you're able to go deeper into your craft and watch your momentum grow fast.

I'm truly excited to take you on this journey of self-discovery and success. Alongside *Create Don't Capture*, you now have everything you need to achieve your goals, build an audience of loyal fans, and scale your business predictably and profitably. Let's explore how this works.

HOW TO USE THIS JOURNAL

THIS JOURNAL FOLLOWS a process that I use every day to gain clarity, be more intentional about my work as a creator and entrepreneur, and optimize myself for peak performance. Each day has a series of prompts and questions for you to answer. I personally leave my journal by my bed and I spend 5–10 minutes on it every night before going to sleep, and 5–10 minutes in the morning right after waking up.

This journal has six months worth of entries in it. If you commit to this process for six months, it should be enough time for you to start seeing incredible results in your life and in your content. But if you're enjoying the process, feel free to start over again from day one in a new journal.

LET'S BREAK DOWN EACH PART OF THE PROCESS:

MORNING

In the morning directly after waking up, do the following:

Morning Prompt

Each morning you'll have a new prompt or question for you to answer in a few sentences. These prompts are designed to do a few things:

1. Give you clarity on who you are, what makes you unique, and how you can provide value
2. Spark ideas for content creation that shows your thought leadership and expertise
3. Start your day right by priming your mind with deep writing and thinking

Simply let yourself write with a stream of consciousness and without editing. There are no right or wrong answers to these questions. Just write whatever comes to mind first. Sometimes you may not even end up answering the question in the prompt, and that is okay. Your mind will lead you where it needs to go.

These prompts are not only designed for your personal development, but they should also spark ideas for content creation. As a creator, when you share your true beliefs, opinions, knowledge, and values in your content, you build credibility and connection with your audience.

This process will kick you into a creative flow that will create a positive impact on the rest of your day.

Creative Flow

Directly after finishing your morning prompt, start your day with a 3–4 hour creative flow session. It's been proven that in the morning after waking up is when our minds are best primed for getting into a flow state and doing deep, productive work.

Before checking social media or getting caught in your emails, get your most demanding, highest-value work done during this window of optimal brain performance. Block this time off from you calendar, move all your meetings to the afternoon, and let your partner and team know that this is sacred time when you are not to be disturbed. Ideally, choose one single intention for this time, and go deep on it.

This is time for you to spend on valuable, high-leverage work that will make a big impact on your life and your business. Whatever you do, don't spend this time in meetings, consuming social media, or doing monotonous day-to-day tasks. Those things will kill creative flow fast.

Here are some activities you might do during this time:

- Writing and creating content
- High level business strategy
- Learning new skills
- Working ON your business
- Writing copy and creating offers
- Networking and making connections

When you do this on a daily basis, you'll find that you can get more done in three hours a day than most people do in 40 hours a week. And in some cases, you might be able to run your entire business in just three hours a day, which frees you up to spend the rest of your time living life on your terms.

At the end of your creative flow session, your mind will likely be exhausted. Deep creative work is some of the most taxing work you can do on your brain, but it is also extremely fulfilling and satisfying. After you finish your session, take a quick walk, eat lunch, listen to a podcast, or do another relaxing activity to reset your brain and prepare you for the rest of the day. If necessary, use the rest of the day to attend meetings, get tasks done, and tie up any loose ends.

EVENING

In the evening, directly before going to sleep, do the following:

Offload

Start by writing down anything that is on your brain that needs to be shelved for tomorrow. This can be anything that you're excited about, or is stressing you out, or things that just need to get done. Take the time to write these things down so you can remember them in the morning. Otherwise your brain will spend all night trying to retain this information and think through it, which will disrupt your sleep.

By writing these down, you're telling your brain, "it's okay, these things are all accounted for and will be taken care of tomorrow." This will improve your sleep by removing these items from your present thoughts, which will allow you to rest.

Gratitude/Wins

A creator cannot create from lack. The practice of writing gratitudes or wins from your day has powerful benefits that will affect every aspect of your life. When you write down what you're grateful for, or things that went well during the day, it helps reframe your mindset around your life, and realize that everything is happening *for* you, and not *to* you. When you operate from this abundance mindset, you will find greater clarity, more motivation, better decision-making, and more momentum. This is key for truly creating at the highest level.

Write down 4 or 5 things that you're grateful for or wins that happened during your day. These can be simple; don't overthink it. If you had a rough day, and are struggling to come up with ideas, try thinking of some of the difficult things that happened during the day, and find a way to reframe them as positive. This practice (especially over time) will guide you into a more fulfilling mindset, and train your brain to operate from positivity and abundance.

Intention

Set one intention for your deep work session tomorrow morning. Sometimes you might have two, but ideally you'll focus on just one. By setting this intention right now, you free your brain from having to make difficult decisions in the morning, so you can wake up and get into creative flow right away. Write down the one or two things you will focus on tomorrow.

Tasks

In this space, you can write down any other tasks or to-do items you need to take care of tomorrow. Typically you will take care of these things in the afternoon after your deep work session.

Welcome To The Creator's Journey

You're about to embark on a journey of self-discovery and productivity that will result in greater clarity, massive momentum, and a true alignment of your life, calling, content, and business. I can't wait for you to get started.

DATE: 

MORNING

What's an opinion you have about your industry or your work that you believe a lot of people would disagree with?

EVENING

Offload:

GRATITUDE/WINS:

-
-
-
-
-

TASKS:

-
-
-
-
-

INTENTION:

DATE: 

MORNING

How were you different a year ago than you are now, and what advice would you give to your past self?

EVENING

Offload:

GRATITUDE/WINS:

-
-
-
-
-

TASKS:

-
-
-
-
-

INTENTION:

DATE:

MORNING

What's a piece of advice you frequently give to others but find hard to follow yourself?

EVENING

Offload:

GRATITUDE/WINS:

-
-
-
-
-

TASKS:

-
-
-
-
-

INTENTION:

DATE:

MORNING

What is one thing that really motivates you, and how can you use it to reach your goals?

EVENING

Offload:

GRATITUDE/WINS:

-
-
-
-
-

TASKS:

-
-
-
-
-

INTENTION:

DATE:

MORNING

When was the last time you struggled to fall asleep, and what was keeping you up?

EVENING

Offload:

GRATITUDE/WINS:

-
-
-
-
-

TASKS:

-
-
-
-
-

INTENTION:

DATE:

MORNING

How is the balance between your work and personal life, and what are you doing to maintain it?

EVENING

Offload:

GRATITUDE/WINS:

-
-
-
-
-

TASKS:

-
-
-
-
-

INTENTION:

DATE:

MORNING

What is something that most people in your field of work do wrong, and what should they do differently?

EVENING

Offload:

GRATITUDE/WINS:

-
-
-
-
-

TASKS:

-
-
-
-
-

INTENTION:

MORNING

If you could step into your audience's or clients' shoes, what is the #1 thing you would do first?

EVENING

Offload:

GRATITUDE/WINS:

-
-
-
-
-

TASKS:

-
-
-
-
-

INTENTION:

DATE: 

MORNING

What is the biggest secret to your success that no one really thinks about?

EVENING

Offload:

GRATITUDE/WINS:

-
-
-
-
-

TASKS:

-
-
-
-
-

INTENTION:

MORNING

What one thing could you change in your life or business right now that would eliminate a large number of problems?

EVENING

Offload:

GRATITUDE/WINS:

-
-
-
-
-

TASKS:

-
-
-
-
-

INTENTION:

DATE: 

MORNING

What's one belief that held you back when you were trying to get where you are now?

EVENING

Offload:

GRATITUDE/WINS:

-
-
-
-
-

TASKS:

-
-
-
-
-

INTENTION:

DATE:

MORNING

What lesson did you learn from your business in the last week?

EVENING

Offload:

GRATITUDE/WINS:

-
-
-
-
-

TASKS:

-
-
-
-
-

INTENTION:

DATE:

MORNING

What's a myth in your field that you would debunk if you could?

EVENING

Offload:

GRATITUDE/WINS:

TASKS:

INTENTION:

DATE: 

MORNING

What is a false belief that most beginners have in your industry, and what should they believe instead?

EVENING

Offload:

GRATITUDE/WINS:

-
-
-
-
-

TASKS:

-
-
-
-
-

INTENTION:

DATE:

MORNING

What is a goal that you're working toward right now and what does achieving it mean to you?

EVENING

Offload:

GRATITUDE/WINS:

-
-
-
-
-

TASKS:

-
-
-
-
-

INTENTION:

DATE:

MORNING

What was a major challenge you faced when starting your business, and what did you do to solve it?

EVENING

Offload:

GRATITUDE/WINS:

-
-
-
-
-

TASKS:

-
-
-
-
-

INTENTION:

DATE: 

MORNING

What's a question that you often get asked by people that don't know you or understand what you do?

EVENING

Offload:

GRATITUDE/WINS:

-
-
-
-
-

TASKS:

-
-
-
-
-

INTENTION:

DATE: 

MORNING

What's a decision you made that completely changed your path, and what happened as a result?

EVENING

Offload:

GRATITUDE/WINS:

-
-
-
-
-

TASKS:

-
-
-
-
-

INTENTION:

DATE: 

MORNING

What's something you did recently for fun that brought intense joy and satisfaction to your life?

EVENING

Offload:

GRATITUDE/WINS:

-
-
-
-
-

TASKS:

-
-
-
-
-

INTENTION:

DATE: 

MORNING

Who was a client of yours that got incredible results recently, and what did they do differently than others?

EVENING

Offload:

GRATITUDE/WINS:

-
-
-
-
-

TASKS:

-
-
-
-
-

INTENTION:

DATE: 

MORNING

What is something that people teach in your industry that is harmful?

EVENING

Offload:

GRATITUDE/WINS:

-
-
-
-
-

TASKS:

-
-
-
-
-

INTENTION:

DATE: 

MORNING

What is something extremely difficult that you had to do recently and how did you do it?

EVENING

Offload:

GRATITUDE/WINS:

-
-
-
-
-

TASKS:

-
-
-
-
-

INTENTION:

DATE: 

MORNING

What is a pet peeve of yours that bothers you every time, and why does it mean so much to you?

EVENING

Offload:

GRATITUDE/WINS:

-
-
-
-
-

TASKS:

-
-
-
-
-

INTENTION:

DATE: 

MORNING

When was the last time you let go of a client or customer and why did you do it?

EVENING

Offload:

GRATITUDE/WINS:

-
-
-
-
-

TASKS:

-
-
-
-
-

INTENTION:

DATE:

MORNING

What's a big macro trend you see coming in your industry and what would you recommend doing to capitalize on it?

EVENING

Offload:

GRATITUDE/WINS:

-
-
-
-
-

TASKS:

-
-
-
-
-

INTENTION:

DATE: 

MORNING

What does your daily routine look like and why do you do things that way?

EVENING

Offload:

GRATITUDE/WINS:

-
-
-
-
-

TASKS:

-
-
-
-
-

INTENTION:

DATE: 

MORNING

What is something that many people avoid doing that you think they should do more?

EVENING

Offload:

GRATITUDE/WINS:

-
-
-
-
-

TASKS:

-
-
-
-
-

INTENTION:

DATE:

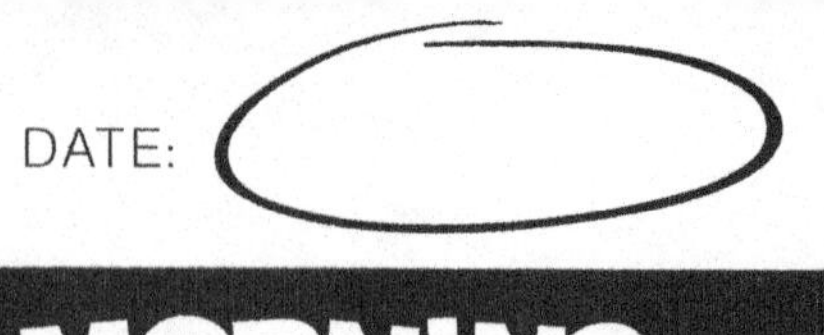

MORNING

What is a belief that you once thought was true but found out it wasn't?

EVENING

Offload:

GRATITUDE/WINS:

-
-
-
-
-

TASKS:

-
-
-
-
-

INTENTION:

DATE: 

MORNING

What's a weird hobby you have that nobody knows about, and why do you choose not to share it?

EVENING

Offload:

GRATITUDE/WINS:

-
-
-
-
-

TASKS:

-
-
-
-
-

INTENTION:

DATE: 

MORNING

Who were you 5 years ago and what questions did you have then about what you currently do now?

EVENING

Offload:

GRATITUDE/WINS:

-
-
-
-
-

TASKS:

-
-
-
-
-

INTENTION:

DATE:

MORNING

What lessondid you learn the hard way?

EVENING

Offload:

GRATITUDE/WINS:

-
-
-
-
-

TASKS:

-
-
-
-
-

INTENTION:

DATE:

MORNING

What is a belief that you had a month ago that you no longer hold?

EVENING

Offload:

GRATITUDE/WINS:

-
-
-
-
-

TASKS:

-
-
-
-
-

INTENTION:

DATE:

MORNING

Who is one of your biggest inspirations in your field and what do you admire about them?

EVENING

Offload:

GRATITUDE/WINS:

-
-
-
-
-

TASKS:

-
-
-
-
-

INTENTION:

DATE:

MORNING

What are you trying to achieve in your life in the next ten years, and why is that important to you?

EVENING

Offload:

GRATITUDE/WINS:

-
-
-
-
-

TASKS:

-
-
-
-
-

INTENTION:

DATE: 

MORNING

What is a big decision you made recently, and what core belief led you to that choice?

EVENING

Offload:

GRATITUDE/WINS:

-
-
-
-
-

TASKS:

-
-
-
-
-

INTENTION:

DATE: 

MORNING

What is one thing that your business does consistently that is a direct reflection of your values?

EVENING

Offload:

GRATITUDE/WINS:

- ■
- ■
- ■
- ■
- ■

TASKS:

- ■
- ■
- ■
- ■
- ■

INTENTION:

DATE: 

MORNING

What is something that you once thought represented success that no longer holds the same meaning?

EVENING

Offload:

GRATITUDE/WINS:

-
-
-
-
-

TASKS:

-
-
-
-
-

INTENTION:

DATE: 

MORNING

What is a lesson you learned from the last time you left your house?

EVENING

Offload:

GRATITUDE/WINS:

-
-
-
-
-

TASKS:

-
-
-
-
-

INTENTION:

DATE:

MORNING

What did you read or listen to recently that impacted you and what lesson did you learn?

EVENING

Offload:

GRATITUDE/WINS:

-
-
-
-
-

TASKS:

-
-
-
-
-

INTENTION:

DATE:

MORNING

What is a question that someone asked you recently in your comments or DMs that you could answer?

EVENING

Offload:

GRATITUDE/WINS:

-
-
-
-
-

TASKS:

-
-
-
-
-

INTENTION:

DATE:

MORNING

What is a commonly held belief in your industry that you would challenge if you had the chance?

EVENING

Offload:

GRATITUDE/WINS:

-
-
-
-
-

TASKS:

-
-
-
-
-

INTENTION:

DATE:

MORNING

What metric do you use to measure success in your life and is there a better one?

EVENING

Offload:

GRATITUDE/WINS:

-
-
-
-
-

TASKS:

-
-
-
-
-

INTENTION:

DATE: 

MORNING

What is the #1 mistake you've seen people making recently and how should they fix it?

EVENING

Offload:

GRATITUDE/WINS:

-
-
-
-
-

TASKS:

-
-
-
-
-

INTENTION:

DATE: 

MORNING

When was a moment that you felt incredibly proud of your work, and what made you feel that?

EVENING

Offload:

GRATITUDE/WINS:

-
-
-
-
-

TASKS:

-
-
-
-
-

INTENTION:

DATE:

MORNING

What's a big risk you took that paid off in a big way?

EVENING

Offload:

GRATITUDE/WINS:

-
-
-
-
-

TASKS:

-
-
-
-
-

INTENTION:

DATE:

MORNING

What is one mistake that you made in your past that you find yourself repeating again now?

EVENING

Offload:

GRATITUDE/WINS:

-
-
-
-
-

TASKS:

-
-
-
-
-

INTENTION:

DATE: 

MORNING

What is a book that significantly influenced your way of thinking and what lessons did you learn from it?

EVENING

Offload:

GRATITUDE/WINS:

■
■
■
■
■

TASKS:

■
■
■
■
■

INTENTION:

DATE: 

MORNING

When was a time that you neglected your personal values to achieve a result in life, and what happened?

EVENING

Offload:

GRATITUDE/WINS:

-
-
-
-
-

TASKS:

-
-
-
-
-

INTENTION:

DATE:

MORNING

What is a problem you're currently solving in your work and what do you think is the path forward?

EVENING

Offload:

GRATITUDE/WINS:

-
-
-
-
-

TASKS:

-
-
-
-
-

INTENTION:

DATE: 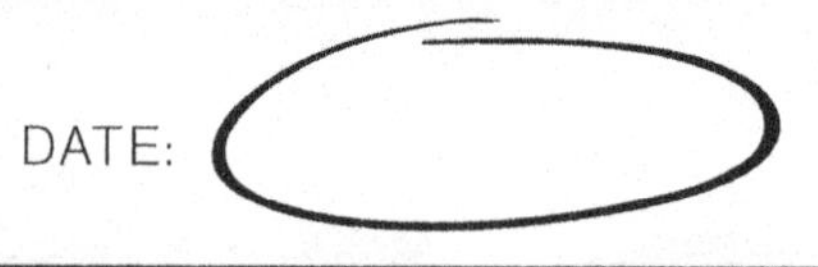

MORNING

What was an extremely difficult client situation you once handled, and what did you learn from it?

EVENING

Offload:

GRATITUDE/WINS:

-
-
-
-
-

TASKS:

-
-
-
-
-

INTENTION:

DATE: 

MORNING

What trend or shift are people missing right now, and what should they do to take advantage of it?

EVENING

Offload:

GRATITUDE/WINS:

-
-
-
-
-

TASKS:

-
-
-
-
-

INTENTION:

DATE: 

MORNING

What is a trending story in the news or in your industry right now and what lesson can you glean from it?

EVENING

Offload:

GRATITUDE/WINS:

-
-
-
-
-

TASKS:

-
-
-
-
-

INTENTION:

DATE: 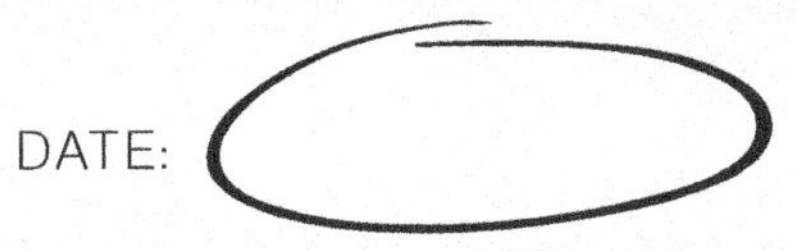

MORNING

What's a question you were asked by someone that you didn't know the answer to?

EVENING

Offload:

GRATITUDE/WINS:

-
-
-
-
-

TASKS:

-
-
-
-
-

INTENTION:

DATE: 

MORNING

When was the last time you cried, and what did that experience reveal about you?

EVENING

Offload:

GRATITUDE/WINS:

-
-
-
-
-

TASKS:

-
-
-
-
-

INTENTION:

DATE: 

MORNING

What's a fun fact about you that most people don't know, and what would happen if they did?

EVENING

Offload:

GRATITUDE/WINS:

-
-
-
-
-

TASKS:

-
-
-
-
-

INTENTION:

DATE: 

MORNING

Who is someone that you've helped make a big change in their life and what did they do?

EVENING

Offload:

GRATITUDE/WINS:

-
-
-
-
-

TASKS:

-
-
-
-
-

INTENTION:

DATE:

MORNING

What is a funny story that happened to you once, and what is the lesson that anyone could take away from it?

EVENING

Offload:

GRATITUDE/WINS:

-
-
-
-
-

TASKS:

-
-
-
-
-

INTENTION:

DATE: 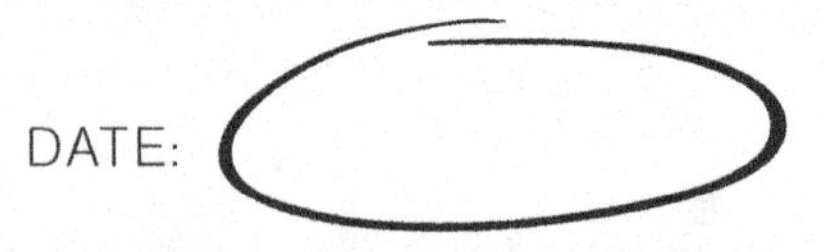

MORNING

What's something big that's happening in your industry right now, and what could you do to be part of it?

EVENING

Offload:

GRATITUDE/WINS:

-
-
-
-
-

TASKS:

-
-
-
-
-

INTENTION:

DATE: 

MORNING

What is a short term decision you've made recently that will have a major impact on the long term vision of your life or business?

EVENING

Offload:

GRATITUDE/WINS:

-
-
-
-
-

TASKS:

-
-
-
-
-

INTENTION:

DATE: 

MORNING

What daily habits have you installed that ensure you are growing and gaining momentum in your life?

EVENING

Offload:

GRATITUDE/WINS:

-
-
-
-
-

TASKS:

-
-
-
-
-

INTENTION:

DATE:

MORNING

What have you done that brought you a significant amount of criticism and how did it shape your beliefs?

EVENING

Offload:

GRATITUDE/WINS:

-
-
-
-
-

TASKS:

-
-
-
-
-

INTENTION:

DATE: 

MORNING

What information do you have that could change someone's life but you rarely get the chance to share it?

EVENING

Offload:

GRATITUDE/WINS:

-
-
-
-
-

TASKS:

-
-
-
-
-

INTENTION:

DATE:

MORNING

What skill are you lacking to get you to the next level, and what could you do right now to develop it?

EVENING

Offload:

GRATITUDE/WINS:

-
-
-
-
-

TASKS:

-
-
-
-
-

INTENTION:

DATE:

MORNING

What experiences in life are you actively trying to avoid that are motivating you to do what you do?

EVENING

Offload:

GRATITUDE/WINS:

-
-
-
-
-

TASKS:

-
-
-
-
-

INTENTION:

DATE: 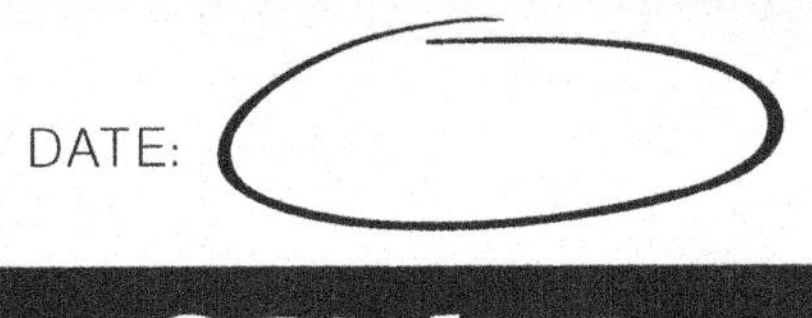

MORNING

What is something that you wouldn't do even if someone offered you money for it, and why?

EVENING

Offload:

GRATITUDE/WINS:

-
-
-
-
-

TASKS:

-
-
-
-
-

INTENTION:

MORNING

What is something that people do to follow the norm that is holding them back in life?

EVENING

Offload:

GRATITUDE/WINS:

-
-
-
-
-

TASKS:

-
-
-
-
-

INTENTION:

DATE:

MORNING

What is one mistake you made in the past that put you in a difficult situation, and what did you do about it?

EVENING

Offload:

GRATITUDE/WINS:

-
-
-
-
-

TASKS:

-
-
-
-
-

INTENTION:

DATE:

MORNING

What is an opinion of yours that you could state that would instantly bring criticism, and what would hold you back from sharing it?

EVENING

Offload:

GRATITUDE/WINS:

-
-
-
-
-

TASKS:

-
-
-
-
-

INTENTION:

DATE:

MORNING

How were you different one month ago than you are right now, and what changed?

EVENING

Offload:

GRATITUDE/WINS:

-
-
-
-
-

TASKS:

-
-
-
-
-

INTENTION:

DATE:

MORNING

What is a value that you know is true, but you still have a hard time living it? Why?

EVENING

Offload:

GRATITUDE/WINS:

-
-
-
-
-

TASKS:

-
-
-
-
-

INTENTION:

DATE: 

MORNING

When was the last time you worked incredibly hard toward a goal and what outcome was motivating you?

EVENING

Offload:

GRATITUDE/WINS:

-
-
-
-
-

TASKS:

-
-
-
-
-

INTENTION:

DATE: 

MORNING

What is something you lost sleep over recently, and how did it impact your life?

EVENING

Offload:

GRATITUDE/WINS:

-
-
-
-
-

TASKS:

-
-
-
-
-

INTENTION:

DATE:

MORNING

When was a time that you neglected balance to go all in on something and what was the outcome, positive or negative?

EVENING

Offload:

GRATITUDE/WINS:

-
-
-
-
-

TASKS:

-
-
-
-
-

INTENTION:

DATE: 

MORNING

What is a bad decision you see people commonly choose in your industry and what should they do instead?

EVENING

Offload:

GRATITUDE/WINS:

-
-
-
-
-

TASKS:

-
-
-
-
-

INTENTION:

DATE:

MORNING

If you could see through your customers' or clients' eyes, what would it change about the approach you're currently taking to your work?

EVENING

Offload:

GRATITUDE/WINS:

-
-
-
-
-

TASKS:

-
-
-
-
-

INTENTION:

DATE:

MORNING

What is a cliche success secret that most people ignore because of its simplicity, and how could it change them?

EVENING

Offload:

GRATITUDE/WINS:

-
-
-
-
-

TASKS:

-
-
-
-
-

INTENTION:

DATE: 

MORNING

What is one thing you could do today that would solve the highest number of issues in your life and business?

EVENING

Offload:

GRATITUDE/WINS:

-
-
-
-
-

TASKS:

-
-
-
-
-

INTENTION:

DATE:

MORNING

When was a time that you got stuck in your business or life, and what belief was keeping you there?

EVENING

Offload:

GRATITUDE/WINS:

-
-
-
-
-

TASKS:

-
-
-
-
-

INTENTION:

DATE:

MORNING

In what way have you leveled up in your life in the last week, and how did you do it?

EVENING

Offload:

GRATITUDE/WINS:

-
-
-
-
-

TASKS:

-
-
-
-
-

INTENTION:

DATE: 

MORNING

What is a lie that is consistently being told in your industry and what is the actual truth?

EVENING

Offload:

GRATITUDE/WINS:

-
-
-
-
-

TASKS:

-
-
-
-
-

INTENTION:

DATE:

MORNING

What is one thing that beginners in your field often do that is not necessary to get them where they want to go, and what should they do instead?

EVENING

Offload:

GRATITUDE/WINS:

-
-
-
-
-

TASKS:

-
-
-
-
-

INTENTION:

MORNING

What is a goal that you want to achieve in one year, and what would you need to do to achieve it in 6 months?

EVENING

Offload:

GRATITUDE/WINS:

-
-
-
-
-

TASKS:

-
-
-
-
-

INTENTION:

DATE: 

MORNING

What was the very first thing you had to learn to start your business, and how would you do it differently now?

EVENING

Offload:

GRATITUDE/WINS:

-
-
-
-
-

TASKS:

-
-
-
-
-

INTENTION:

DATE:

MORNING

What is a question that you've been asked more than once by different people, and what is the answer?

EVENING

Offload:

GRATITUDE/WINS:

-
-
-
-
-

TASKS:

-
-
-
-
-

INTENTION:

DATE:

MORNING

What is something you did that resulted in a huge leap in your life, and how could you replicate that now?

EVENING

Offload:

GRATITUDE/WINS:

-
-
-
-
-

TASKS:

-
-
-
-
-

INTENTION:

DATE:

MORNING

When was the last time you laughed until tears came out of your eyes, and what were you doing in the moment?

EVENING

Offload:

GRATITUDE/WINS:

-
-
-
-
-

TASKS:

-
-
-
-
-

INTENTION:

DATE: 

MORNING

What has made you successful in what you do that other people are failing at?

EVENING

Offload:

GRATITUDE/WINS:

-
-
-
-
-

TASKS:

-
-
-
-
-

INTENTION:

DATE: 

MORNING

What unproductive practices or teachings are other people sharing in your industry that are actually holding people back?

EVENING

Offload:

GRATITUDE/WINS:

- ■
- ■
- ■
- ■
- ■

TASKS:

- ■
- ■
- ■
- ■
- ■

INTENTION:

DATE: 

MORNING

What was a recent situation that gave you a pit in your stomach and how did you end up in that situation?

EVENING

Offload:

GRATITUDE/WINS:

-
-
-
-
-

TASKS:

-
-
-
-
-

INTENTION:

DATE:

MORNING

What is something that you absolutely despise, and why is it so important to you?

EVENING

Offload:

GRATITUDE/WINS:

-
-
-
-
-

TASKS:

-
-
-
-
-

INTENTION:

DATE:

MORNING

What could a client or customer do that would make you consider firing them, and why?

EVENING

Offload:

GRATITUDE/WINS:

-
-
-
-
-

TASKS:

-
-
-
-
-

INTENTION:

DATE: 

MORNING

How will your industry be different 5 years from now, and what should people be doing to prepare?

EVENING

Offload:

GRATITUDE/WINS:

-
-
-
-
-

TASKS:

-
-
-
-
-

INTENTION:

DATE: 

MORNING

What things do you do consistently every day, and how do they impact your life?

EVENING

Offload:

GRATITUDE/WINS:

-
-
-
-
-

TASKS:

-
-
-
-
-

INTENTION:

DATE:

MORNING

What are three to five tools or resources that you use regularly that propel you to your goals faster?

EVENING

Offload:

GRATITUDE/WINS:

-
-
-
-
-

TASKS:

-
-
-
-
-

INTENTION:

DATE: 

MORNING

What is something that you used to tell people that you don't actually believe anymore?

EVENING

Offload:

GRATITUDE/WINS:

-
-
-
-
-

TASKS:

-
-
-
-
-

INTENTION:

DATE:

MORNING

What is something you do regularly that you would be embarrassed if someone found out, and why?

EVENING

Offload:

GRATITUDE/WINS:

-
-
-
-
-

TASKS:

-
-
-
-
-

INTENTION:

DATE:

MORNING

What is something that you've neglected in your life in order to achieve something else, and why did you do it?

EVENING

Offload:

GRATITUDE/WINS:

-
-
-
-
-

TASKS:

-
-
-
-
-

INTENTION:

DATE: 

MORNING

What is your audience trying to get away from in life that is motivating them to do what they do?

EVENING

Offload:

GRATITUDE/WINS:

-
-
-
-
-

TASKS:

-
-
-
-
-

DATE:

MORNING

When did failure teach you a lesson that you will never forget?

EVENING

Offload:

GRATITUDE/WINS:

-
-
-
-
-

TASKS:

-
-
-
-
-

INTENTION:

DATE: 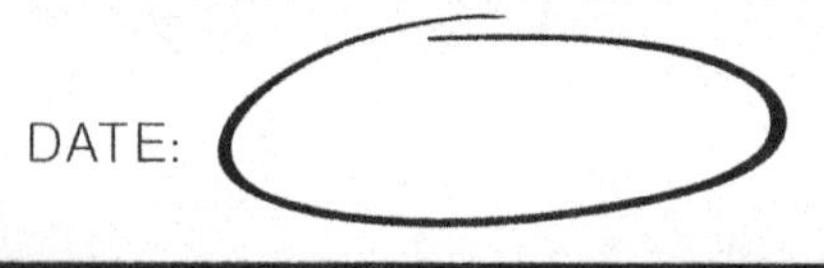

MORNING

What is something that was extremely important to you a month ago that isn't any longer?

EVENING

Offload:

GRATITUDE/WINS:

-
-
-
-
-

TASKS:

-
-
-
-
-

INTENTION:

DATE:

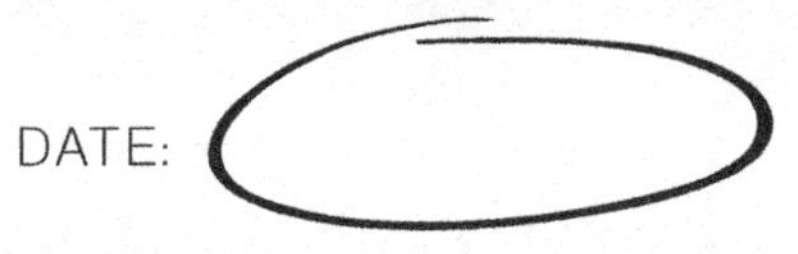

MORNING

Who is the top expert in your industry and what is one thing they do that most people don't?

EVENING

Offload:

GRATITUDE/WINS:

-
-
-
-
-

TASKS:

-
-
-
-
-

INTENTION:

DATE: 

MORNING

If you could achieve one thing in the next ten years, what would it be and what would it mean to you?

EVENING

Offload:

GRATITUDE/WINS:

-
-
-
-
-

TASKS:

-
-
-
-
-

INTENTION:

DATE:

MORNING

What is a decision you made between two equally valuable options, and what internal belief led you to choose the one you did?

EVENING

Offload:

GRATITUDE/WINS:

-
-
-
-
-

TASKS:

-
-
-
-
-

INTENTION:

DATE:

MORNING

What is a decision that you made in your business recently that put your values on display?

EVENING

Offload:

GRATITUDE/WINS:

-
-
-
-
-

TASKS:

-
-
-
-
-

INTENTION:

DATE: 

MORNING

How long ago do you have to go back to find a time when you thought your current success was impossible, and what did you believe back then?

EVENING

Offload:

GRATITUDE/WINS:

-
-
-
-
-

TASKS:

-
-
-
-
-

INTENTION:

DATE: 

MORNING

What is an object in your room that means something to you and what lesson could other people learn from it?

EVENING

Offload:

GRATITUDE/WINS:

-
-
-
-
-

TASKS:

-
-
-
-
-

INTENTION:

DATE: 

MORNING

What's a piece advice you heard or received recently that could make a big impact on someone else?

EVENING

Offload:

GRATITUDE/WINS:

-
-
-
-
-

TASKS:

-
-
-
-
-

INTENTION:

DATE: 

MORNING

What question do people often ask who are beginners in your industry, and what question should they be asking instead?

EVENING

Offload:

GRATITUDE/WINS:

-
-
-
-
-

TASKS:

-
-
-
-
-

INTENTION:

DATE:

MORNING

What is one thing that a major influencer in your space teaches that you believe is wrong, and why?

EVENING

Offload:

GRATITUDE/WINS:

-
-
-
-
-

TASKS:

-
-
-
-
-

INTENTION:

DATE: 

MORNING

What success have you achieved recently and what indicator did you use to determine it was a success?

EVENING

Offload:

GRATITUDE/WINS:

TASKS:

INTENTION:

DATE:

MORNING

What is something most people get wrong about your industry and what should they think instead?

EVENING

Offload:

GRATITUDE/WINS:

-
-
-
-
-

TASKS:

-
-
-
-
-

INTENTION:

DATE: 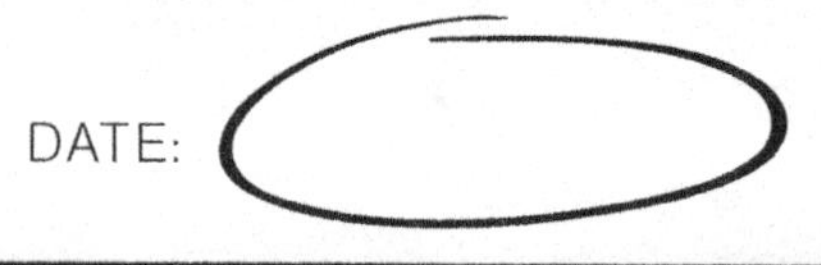

MORNING

What is something that you feel proud of for achieving, and what did it take to get there?

EVENING

Offload:

GRATITUDE/WINS:

-
-
-
-
-

TASKS:

-
-
-
-
-

INTENTION:

DATE:

MORNING

What's something you did that people thought was crazy but it actually got you where you needed to go?

EVENING

Offload:

GRATITUDE/WINS:

-
-
-
-
-

TASKS:

-
-
-
-
-

INTENTION:

DATE: 

MORNING

What habits are you currently doing that are prohibiting your growth and what should you replace them with?

EVENING

Offload:

GRATITUDE/WINS:

-
-
-
-
-

TASKS:

-
-
-
-
-

INTENTION:

DATE: 

MORNING

What book have you read recently that completely changed your paradigm on something, and what did it say?

EVENING

Offload:

GRATITUDE/WINS:

-
-
-
-
-

TASKS:

-
-
-
-
-

INTENTION:

DATE:

MORNING

When was a time that you did something you're not proud of, and it worked out in your favor?

EVENING

Offload:

GRATITUDE/WINS:

-
-
-
-
-

TASKS:

-
-
-
-
-

INTENTION:

DATE: 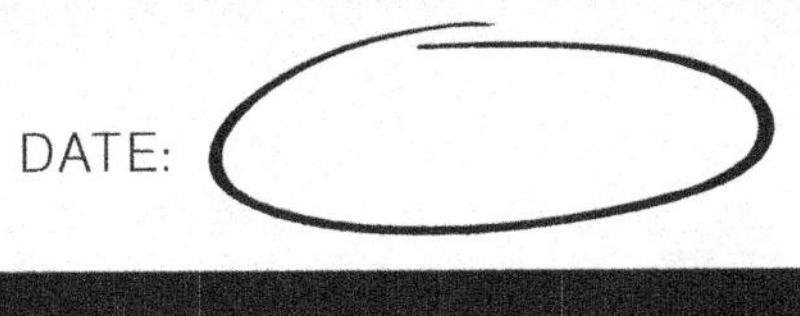

MORNING

What is something that you'd be embarrassed if your audience found out about you, and how do you think they would respond?

EVENING

Offload:

GRATITUDE/WINS:

-
-
-
-
-

TASKS:

-
-
-
-
-

INTENTION:

DATE: 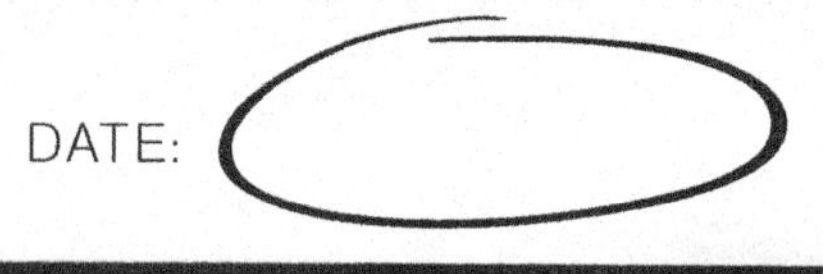

MORNING

What is currently stopping you from getting to the next level, and what is the simplest path through it that you can think of?

EVENING

Offload:

GRATITUDE/WINS:

-
-
-
-
-

TASKS:

-
-
-
-
-

INTENTION:

DATE:

MORNING

What was a difficult experience you had with an employee or co-worker and how did you handle it?

EVENING

Offload:

GRATITUDE/WINS:

-
-
-
-
-

TASKS:

-
-
-
-
-

INTENTION:

DATE: 

MORNING

What is something that pioneers in your industry are working on right now that most people still don't know about?

EVENING

Offload:

GRATITUDE/WINS:

-
-
-
-
-

TASKS:

-
-
-
-
-

INTENTION:

DATE:

MORNING

What current news or event are people in your field talking about and what are they getting wrong about it?

EVENING

Offload:

GRATITUDE/WINS:

-
-
-
-
-

TASKS:

-
-
-
-
-

INTENTION:

DATE:

MORNING

What's a piece of advice that someone has given you that actually turned out to be wrong?

EVENING

Offload:

GRATITUDE/WINS:

-
-
-
-
-

TASKS:

-
-
-
-
-

INTENTION:

DATE:

MORNING

What's something you've never told anyone about yourself, and what would happen if you did?

EVENING

Offload:

GRATITUDE/WINS:

-
-
-
-
-

TASKS:

-
-
-
-
-

INTENTION:

DATE:

MORNING

Who is someone that has thanked you for your help and what did you help them with that could be valuable to other people?

EVENING

Offload:

GRATITUDE/WINS:

-
-
-
-
-

TASKS:

-
-
-
-
-

INTENTION:

DATE: 

MORNING

What is something you did to grow your business that other people would find funny?

EVENING

Offload:

GRATITUDE/WINS:

-
-
-
-
-

TASKS:

-
-
-
-
-

INTENTION:

DATE:

MORNING

What is trending in your industry right now and how could you capitalize on it?

EVENING

Offload:

GRATITUDE/WINS:

-
-
-
-
-

TASKS:

-
-
-
-
-

INTENTION:

DATE: 

MORNING

What is a decision you made recently that prioritized your long term vision over short term gains, and what was the result?

EVENING

Offload:

GRATITUDE/WINS:

-
-
-
-
-

TASKS:

-
-
-
-
-

INTENTION:

DATE:

MORNING

What is one thing that you've done every single day for the last year, and what motivated you to stay consistent with it?

EVENING

Offload:

GRATITUDE/WINS:

-
-
-
-
-

TASKS:

-
-
-
-
-

INTENTION:

DATE:

MORNING

What is one thing that someone has criticized you for and how did it affect your actions going forward?

EVENING

Offload:

GRATITUDE/WINS:

-
-
-
-
-

TASKS:

-
-
-
-
-

INTENTION:

DATE: 

MORNING

Who do you know that you would give advice to, but you'll probably never have the chance?

EVENING

Offload:

GRATITUDE/WINS:

-
-
-
-
-

TASKS:

-
-
-
-
-

INTENTION:

DATE: 

MORNING

What habit are you doing right now that is holding you back from getting to where you want to go, and what would it take to change it?

EVENING

Offload:

GRATITUDE/WINS:

-
-
-
-
-

TASKS:

-
-
-
-
-

INTENTION:

DATE: 

MORNING

What actions are you taking in your business currently to avoid something negative?

EVENING

Offload:

GRATITUDE/WINS:

-
-
-
-
-

TASKS:

-
-
-
-
-

INTENTION:

DATE: 

MORNING

What is something that has been asked of you and you said no, and what led that decision?

EVENING

Offload:

GRATITUDE/WINS:

-
-
-
-
-

TASKS:

-
-
-
-
-

INTENTION:

DATE:

MORNING

When was a time that you failed miserably at something, but it actually turned into a success?

EVENING

Offload:

GRATITUDE/WINS:

-
-
-
-
-

TASKS:

-
-
-
-
-

INTENTION:

DATE:

MORNING

What is something you read recently that made you think about something in a different way?

EVENING

Offload:

GRATITUDE/WINS:

-
-
-
-
-

TASKS:

-
-
-
-
-

INTENTION:

DATE: 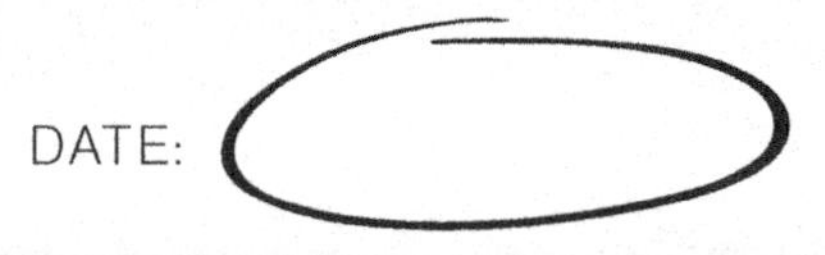

MORNING

What is something that is currently trending in your industry that you don't think is worth paying attention to?

EVENING

Offload:

GRATITUDE/WINS:

-
-
-
-
-

TASKS:

-
-
-
-
-

INTENTION:

DATE: 

MORNING

Who in your space recently had a successful campaign and what lesson could you teach from it?

EVENING

Offload:

GRATITUDE/WINS:

TASKS:

INTENTION:

DATE: 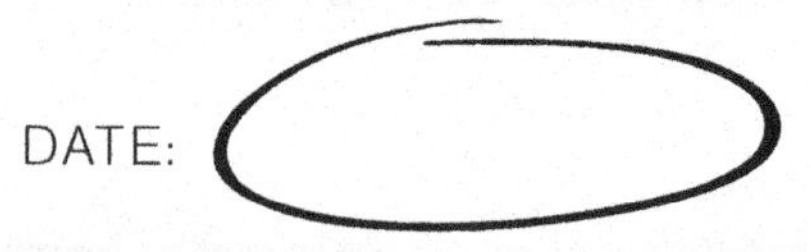

MORNING

What is something that people often do wrong without realizing they're doing it?

EVENING

Offload:

GRATITUDE/WINS:

-
-
-
-
-

TASKS:

-
-
-
-
-

INTENTION:

DATE:

MORNING

If you could take someone to exactly where you are now in three steps, what would those three steps be?

EVENING

Offload:

GRATITUDE/WINS:

■

■

■

■

■

TASKS:

■

■

■

■

■

INTENTION:

DATE: 

MORNING

What was a successful project you completed recently and what steps should someone take to replicate it?

EVENING

Offload:

GRATITUDE/WINS:

-
-
-
-
-

TASKS:

-
-
-
-
-

INTENTION:

DATE: 

MORNING

What are three tools that you couldn't operate without, and how would you work differently if you didn't have them?

EVENING

Offload:

GRATITUDE/WINS:

-
-
-
-
-

TASKS:

-
-
-
-
-

INTENTION:

DATE:

MORNING

What is the story behind the name of your business and what does it say about you?

EVENING

Offload:

GRATITUDE/WINS:

TASKS:

INTENTION:

DATE: 

MORNING

Where did you go on your most recent vacation and why did you choose that place over somewhere else?

EVENING

Offload:

GRATITUDE/WINS:

-
-
-
-
-

TASKS:

-
-
-
-
-

INTENTION:

DATE: 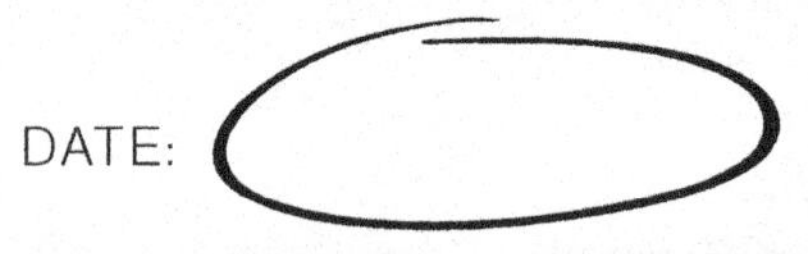

MORNING

What is one thing you often do in your spare time that is hugely beneficial to your life?

EVENING

Offload:

GRATITUDE/WINS:

-
-
-
-
-

TASKS:

-
-
-
-
-

INTENTION:

DATE:

MORNING

What one mistake do you see people making right now that you firmly believe should be changed, and what should they do instead?

EVENING

Offload:

GRATITUDE/WINS:

-
-
-
-
-

TASKS:

-
-
-
-
-

INTENTION:

DATE: 

MORNING

What's the most challenging question you've ever received from a follower or customer?

EVENING

Offload:

GRATITUDE/WINS:

-
-
-
-
-

TASKS:

-
-
-
-
-

INTENTION:

DATE: 

MORNING

When was an unexpected turning point in your career that resulted in a surprising amount of success?

EVENING

Offload:

GRATITUDE/WINS:

-
-
-
-
-

TASKS:

-
-
-
-
-

INTENTION:

DATE:

MORNING

Who else in your industry has been through similar struggles to you and what did they do different to solve them?

EVENING

Offload:

GRATITUDE/WINS:

TASKS:

INTENTION:

DATE: 

MORNING

What mistake did you make six months ago that put you in your current situation, and what will you do differently to get out of it in the next six months?

EVENING

Offload:

GRATITUDE/WINS:

-
-
-
-
-

TASKS:

-
-
-
-
-

INTENTION:

DATE: 

MORNING

What is an event in history that shaped the way you think about your work?

EVENING

Offload:

GRATITUDE/WINS:

-
-
-
-
-

TASKS:

-
-
-
-
-

INTENTION:

DATE: 

MORNING

What is one problem you're currently trying to solve in your life, and how are you going about it wrong?

EVENING

Offload:

GRATITUDE/WINS:

-
-
-
-
-

TASKS:

-
-
-
-
-

INTENTION:

DATE: 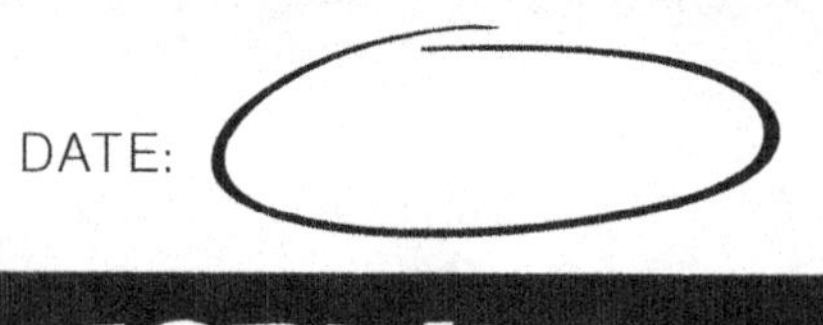

MORNING

What is a common misconception in your industry that you always feel like you're having to correct?

EVENING

Offload:

GRATITUDE/WINS:

-
-
-
-
-

TASKS:

-
-
-
-
-

INTENTION:

DATE: 

MORNING

What is a difficult decision you made recently and what process did you follow to come to the conclusion?

EVENING

Offload:

GRATITUDE/WINS:

-
-
-
-
-

TASKS:

-
-
-
-
-

INTENTION:

DATE: 

MORNING

When have you experienced a spectacular failure that actually turned into a positive outcome?

EVENING

Offload:

GRATITUDE/WINS:

-
-
-
-
-

TASKS:

-
-
-
-
-

INTENTION:

DATE:

MORNING

What will people be talking about in your industry in five years, and what can you be doing now to be part of it?

EVENING

Offload:

GRATITUDE/WINS:

-
-
-
-
-

TASKS:

-
-
-
-
-

INTENTION:

DATE:

MORNING

What is the biggest outcome you're looking for in your life and work, and why do you care about it so much?

EVENING

Offload:

GRATITUDE/WINS:

-
-
-
-
-

TASKS:

-
-
-
-
-

INTENTION:

DATE:

MORNING

What change has happened in your field in the last year and how did you change to accommodate it?

EVENING

Offload:

GRATITUDE/WINS:

TASKS:

INTENTION:

DATE: 

MORNING

What does an average day look like for you and what's one thing you could change about it to make it better?

EVENING

Offload:

GRATITUDE/WINS:

-
-
-
-
-

TASKS:

-
-
-
-
-

INTENTION:

DATE:

MORNING

How would you describe the life you don't want and why don't you want it?

EVENING

Offload:

GRATITUDE/WINS:

-
-
-
-
-

TASKS:

-
-
-
-
-

INTENTION:

DATE:

MORNING

When was a time that you rejected a job or payment and what was the motivating factor behind it?

EVENING

Offload:

GRATITUDE/WINS:

-
-
-
-
-

TASKS:

-
-
-
-
-

INTENTION:

DATE: 

MORNING

If you had completely financial security starting right now, what would you spend the next 24 hours doing?

EVENING

Offload:

GRATITUDE/WINS:

-
-
-
-
-

TASKS:

-
-
-
-
-

INTENTION:

DATE: 

MORNING

What is something that some people dislike about you that you love about yourself?

EVENING

Offload:

GRATITUDE/WINS:

-
-
-
-
-

TASKS:

-
-
-
-
-

INTENTION:

DATE: 

MORNING

When was a time that you threw away something important to you in order to achieve a short term goal?

EVENING

Offload:

GRATITUDE/WINS:

-
-
-
-
-

TASKS:

-
-
-
-
-

INTENTION:

DATE:

MORNING

If you were the CEO of your customers' business, what changes would you enact immediately to see the biggest results fast?

EVENING

Offload:

GRATITUDE/WINS:

-
-
-
-
-

TASKS:

-
-
-
-
-

INTENTION:

DATE: 

MORNING

What is a success secret that everyone talks about but nobody really does? What would happen if they did?

EVENING

Offload:

GRATITUDE/WINS:

-
-
-
-
-

TASKS:

-
-
-
-
-

INTENTION:

DATE: 

MORNING

If you had to eliminate 90% of your tasks this week, which ones would you delete and why?

EVENING

Offload:

GRATITUDE/WINS:

-
-
-
-
-

TASKS:

-
-
-
-
-

INTENTION:

DATE: 

MORNING

What do you hope to have happen at the end of this month and what could you do to make it happen by the end of this week?

EVENING

Offload:

GRATITUDE/WINS:

-
-
-
-
-

TASKS:

-
-
-
-
-

INTENTION:

DATE:

MORNING

Who is someone that makes you happy every time you're around them and what is it about them that makes you feel that way?

EVENING

Offload:

GRATITUDE/WINS:

-
-
-
-
-

TASKS:

-
-
-
-
-

INTENTION:

DATE:

MORNING

What character trait do you naturally have that has made you successful that other people lack?

EVENING

Offload:

GRATITUDE/WINS:

-
-
-
-
-

TASKS:

-
-
-
-
-

INTENTION:

DATE: 

MORNING

How are you a different person than you were twenty four hours ago, and what has changed?

EVENING

Offload:

GRATITUDE/WINS:

-
-
-
-
-

TASKS:

-
-
-
-
-

INTENTION:

DATE:

MORNING

What is the question you could ask someone right now and the correct answer would solve a majority of issues in your life?

EVENING

Offload:

GRATITUDE/WINS:

-
-
-
-
-

TASKS:

-
-
-
-
-

INTENTION:

DATE:

MORNING

What is something that made you angry recently and what did that experience uncover about you and your values?

EVENING

Offload:

GRATITUDE/WINS:

-
-
-
-
-

TASKS:

-
-
-
-
-

INTENTION:

DATE: 

MORNING

If you could simplify your success in life so far down to one single habit, what would it be?

EVENING

Offload:

GRATITUDE/WINS:

-
-
-
-
-

TASKS:

-
-
-
-
-

INTENTION:

DATE: 

MORNING

Over the last six months of writing in this journal, what is the one biggest thing you've discovered about yourself and the one biggest shift you've made as a result? What will you do for the next 6 months to apply it going forward?

EVENING

Offload:

GRATITUDE/WINS:

-
-
-
-
-

TASKS:

-
-
-
-
-

INTENTION:

ADDITIONAL NOTES:

ADDITIONAL NOTES:

ADDITIONAL NOTES:

ADDITIONAL NOTES:

ADDITIONAL NOTES:

Made in the USA
Monee, IL
28 April 2025

16517343R00115